SUSTAINABLE
Spirituality
GUIDEBOOK

TODD RODARMEL

Cover design and layout by Ryan Kirkland | @ryan.creating (dearryan@me.com)
Cover photo by Peter Hershey | peterhershey.com | @peterhershey

For wholesale pricing and bulk orders, email: Todd@mvc.life

TABLE OF CONTENTS

LOVE FOR EACH PERSON

RESTORATION OF ALL THINGS

SO WHAT'S NEXT?   *133*

EXTRAS   *139*

FOREWORD

I woke up just as the camp speaker was calling every-one forward to give their lives to Jesus. It's not clear to me just when I fell asleep. All I remember is hearing about how painful crucifixion was as a method of tor-ture and execution. (Also, honestly how painful my butt was from sitting for so long on the hard floor.)

Three or four days into camp the schedule has a way of catching up to you. Late nights messing around in the cabin and early mornings singing in the chapel set up sleep deprived kids for exhaustion by the middle of the week. Team competitions during recreation time and endless adventures during free time tax the body. Deep talks at chapel times and late night discussions in small groups bring the emotional and mental fatigue in line with the physical.

On that night in the summer of 1982, an exhausted thirteen year old boy woke up at just the right time to receive Jesus. Though minutes before he was in dream land; though hours before he was more concerned about meeting girls; though days before he called his mom to come pick him up because he felt out of place and alone; at just the right time, he woke up and went forward. The course of my life was changed forever.

My heart was changed. I wanted to know God. The Bible came alive to me. My friend group changed. Pri-orities changed. Though I wasn't always good, at least now I wanted to be! My whole being wanted to know God and love God and serve God for the rest of my life. It's still funny to me that such a born again experience can happen out of a dead sleep. But it did. It was supernatural and the beginning of a life calling that led me into ministry for all the years since.

As a youth pastor I led others on camps for many years and took part in programming these transformative experiences. We knew just how to move kids to the point of decision and how to set structures in place to follow up on their decisions. But each year I would notice a pattern. After camp, kids would be on fire for a few weeks or months and eventually cool off into complacency. So we would soon have another camp or mission trip to reignite the fire. Their spiritual lives depended on the schedule of our ministry year to keep them going.

The problem is that this kind of external stimulus can only be kept up for so long. Kids graduate. They go to college. Adults don't have time to go on three or four trips a year to keep the fire going. Something needs to be done to make people's relationship with God more sustainable in the long term.

In fact, something was needed in my own spirituality to make it sustainable. Sunday services, Bible studies and accountability groups were not enough. These outward supports were good for worship, learning and friendship, but if I was going to sustain my relationship with God, it would have to come from the inside out.

All sustainable spirituality is from the inside out. We don't have camp directors and speakers every day in our lives. It puts unattainable pressure on our churches to expect them to provide us all we need to sustain a life of faith. What we need is to learn to take responsibility for ourselves. We must be honest with where we are, build an intimate relationship with God, cultivate an actual (not forced) love for each person and have a vision that calls us to be part of the restoration God is bringing on earth.

That is what I have developed personally and what I have worked to create at Mountain View Church for the last 20 years. This workbook is a guide to help people, both in and outside our church cultivate a sustainable spirituality. It can be used alone or in groups, but community is always the best context for sustained growth.

The community that helped me create this was made up of some amazing friends. My wife Traci Rodarmel added her years of experience in the classroom to many of the exercises. My son Zac Rodarmel brought his prophetic insights to bear in the writing and development of the ideas. Ryan Kirkland did a masterful job with the layout and publishing. Bob Mattson was an invaluable help with the editing. The whole project would not have happened without the writing, project management, and constant pushing forward of Drew Tilton. More than anyone else, he is the heart behind this project. I'm so thankful for the great team God has given me.

As the old African proverb goes, "If you want to go fast, go alone. If you want to go far, go together." My prayer is that this guidebook goes far in helping you and your companions build a sustainable spirituality. Enjoy this guide as our gift to you and give us feedback about what is helpful and what is not. We are committed to improving this material to be useful for as many people as possible far into the future.

Hopeful,

Todd Rodarmel

INTRODUCTION

CULTIVATING SUSTAINABLE SPIRITUALITY

SUSTAINABLE

You can probably point to one or more times in your life when you encountered God in an especially meaningful way. It might have been at a camp, conference, retreat or similar setting. If you're like most of us, however, the spiritual high you experienced at those special times didn't last once you returned to your everyday world.

So how do you continue the mountain top experience in your spiritual life? You don't. The reality is that staying on fire constantly burns up resources and eventually burns you out. What is better is a sustainable life with God.

Serving God and laying down your life for others is a noble vision for life. But if you are not refilling the reservoir of your soul, the depletion associated with those efforts will eventually bleed you dry.

What's needed is a way of life in which your tank is being continually filled by God's Spirit. That way, the abundance being produced in and through your life can bless others without depleting you.

Like a faucet that's constantly pouring into a glass, God wants his Spirit to continually pour into and fill your life, producing an overflow from which you can serve others. You then find yourself able to give from his unlimited resources as opposed to your finite energy and abilities. This is the secret to a lifetime of abundance for yourself and others.

Sustainability has been described as giving more than you take. What if your life was characterized by God's abundant and continual blessing overflowing from you into the lives of others in a sustainable fashion? Would you believe this is possible?

SPIRITUALITY

Simply defined, spirituality is about how you live in relationship with God. It's not the same as religion or even faith. It's about the ability of your soul to breathe.

In both of the languages the Bible was written in, "spirit", "breath" and "wind" are the same word. The idea carries over into our language when you think about what is "inspiring" or "expiring".

To be spiritual is to be connected to the breath of God. He is always closer than the air. When we are conscious of our connection to God, it is like paying attention to our breath. Singers get this. Yogis get this. Runners get this.

When we look for inspiration only in the sporadic and infrequent connection to God that we enjoy "on the mountain top", we undervalue the ordinary, everyday ways that God is present in and with us.

What if you could find God's presence in your daily moments of work, rest, play, eating, sleeping, breathing and connecting with others? What if you could see God as not being so much interested in your religious activities as he is with every detail of your life?

What if the fact of God's loving presence with you influenced every moment of your life?

CULTIVATING

Growing spiritually doesn't happen overnight. People grow and change over time. That's why Jesus told so many stories that revolved around farming. Farming is a slow, organic process.

The farmer sows the seed like God speaks to us. Just as the condition of the soil determines the effect of the farmer's sown seed, the condition and receptivity of our hearts determines how we respond to what God says to us.

The Kingdom of God begins like mustard seed, initially small and undetected. Yet, as it takes root, it grows and flourishes, spreading until it takes over the whole earth.

A good tree bears good fruit; an unhealthy tree produces bad fruit or no fruit at all. The only way to produce good fruit is to grow and sustain a healthy tree. That is true in our spiritual lives as well. Jesus is the vine; we are the branches. If we stay connected to him and his life flows through us, we will bear good fruit as well.

Over and over Jesus is telling us that our spiritual lives work naturally according to principles of God's Spirit.

It is a process that starts with God's Spirit transforming us from the inside out and then having us move out into the world. It doesn't work if you skip steps or work from the outside in. Just like the glass needs to be filled before an overflow can happen, we need to be filled with God's Spirit first before we can bless others as he intended.

So how does that work practically? In short, it starts with an honest look at yourself that leads to a genuine pursuit of intimacy with God. Then, as you love the people around you with his love, it eventually leads to the restoration of all things.

We will be exploring this process in depth over the next eight weeks. But first let's look at how this guidebook is designed to help you and your group.

HOW THIS GUIDEBOOK WORKS

Sustainable Spirituality is not just a book or curriculum. Rather, it is an eight week journey you will travel with God and others to cultivate a sustainable spirituality in your life. This book is designed to guide you around four core values that shaped the life of Jesus and define the process of spiritual transformation.

We will spend two weeks exploring each value in depth. The first meeting you spend exploring each value will be more conversation based, while the second meeting will be more experience based. Here is a breakdown of each value:

WEEK 1 & 2
AUTHENTICITY WITH SELF is the starting point. If you don't know where you are, you are lost. The honest assessment of your strengths and your shortcomings is the first step in your journey to the abundant life and a real, sustainable spirituality. If you can't be real with

yourself, you will be limited in your ability to bring anything real and worthwhile to others.

WEEK 3 & 4
INTIMACY WITH GOD is the way to get beyond yourself. You were created for a relationship with God and you will have an unfillable hole in your life without him. When you learn to trust God and listen to the voice of the Holy Spirit, your life will change in important ways. You will be able to live at a supernatural level most people don't realize is possible. Resources you didn't imagine you had access to will suddenly be available to you. Best of all, peace and grace will be yours as you practice the way of Jesus.

WEEK 5 & 6
LOVE FOR EACH PERSON is not just a command from the Bible, like something you are supposed to do. It is a gift from God by the Holy Spirit that you can actually have. God's own love can reorient your life to actually love people you may not even like on your own. You can love each person like your own flesh and blood. Part practice and part gift, this will truly change your life as your heart begins to reflect the heart of God. How you respond to your everyday encounters with each person in your life reveals your true spirituality.

WEEK 7 & 8
THE RESTORATION OF ALL THINGS is God's dream for the world. The one who created everything wants to see it come to fruition. God's plan for the world is not to destroy it but to redeem every aspect of it. From ecology to economics, from arts to astrophysics, from business to building, and from laundromats to law firms, Jesus is making all things new. Your goal becomes finding your role in his restoration project.

GROUP EXPERIENCE:
YOUR TIME TOGETHER

Each week you will meet with your group. There will be a short reading to introduce the topic with either questions to discuss or an activity to do together. Though some of your groups may have a facilitator, this guide is written so that you can learn together without one. You can simply take turns reading the introductions and asking the questions.

DEVOTIONS:
YOUR PERSONAL TIME

Between meetings, there are personal readings, prayer exercises, and questions for reflection that we call devotions. Devotions will enhance your experience and help you dig further into the ideas discussed in your group. These devotions are short but important. If you want to get the most out of this experience, we recommend you engage with these personal readings and experiences. Give the prayer practices a try, look up the Bible verses, journal your reflections, be bold and allow God to stretch you. You'll be glad you did. Each devotion is short enough that you can complete it in ten minutes, but rich enough that you could make an hour out of it. It's up to you.

Ready? Let's go.

Authenticity
WITH SELF

WEEK 1 **GETTING REAL**

The starting point for true spirituality is authenticity with self. That's because you can only start where you are. So, where are you right now? *Honestly?*

Don't be afraid of the good and the bad of who you are. It's you. You have amazing gifts and ways that you reflect the image of God. You also have horrible ways you have distorted that image. Give up trying to fake it. Have the courage it takes to live honestly in the reality of your broken human experience.

Too many people spend their lives trying to appear to others as different than who they really are (or think they are). What if you chose to become the person Christ always designed you to be and stopped pretending and hiding? If you were completely accepted as you are and you could do nothing to lose that acceptance, how would your life be different? *What if you already are that accepted?*

The Bible tells us we were created in the image of God, (Gen. 1:27) but we have all sinned and fallen short of that image. (Rom. 3:23) True spirituality admits that as a starting point. Creation in the image of God is our primary identity as humans. The reality that we have all sinned doesn't change that fact. Sin distorts the image. It doesn't erase it.

The beauty of the new covenant revealed in and inaugurated through Jesus is that by faith in him sinners become saints. This change of identity is central to your ability to live the abundant life. It will be impossible to live like a saint if you see yourself as a sinner. It will also be impossible to call out the best in others if you believe the truest thing about them is their sin and depravity.

Many Christians are stuck in patterns of sin because they believe they are and will always be sinners, that their hearts are wicked, and that there is nothing good in them. So they keep acting like sinners. They believe they are JUST forgiven sinners, covered with the righteousness of Jesus, but not truly good in any sense of the term. This view is based on a total misunderstanding of the Bible and the meaning of the new covenant.

The Bible says that we were created in the image of God with incredible value to him and capacity for good. (Gen. 1:26, Psalm 8:5-6, Eph. 2:10) Our sin doesn't change that. After all, Christ died for us *while* we were still sinners. However, the Bible also takes seriously the fact that we are all deeply flawed and in need of redemption. (Romans 3:23) We have all fallen short of the glory God intended for us to display as the bearers of his image, but we are each so valuable to God that he leaves the ninety-nine to go after the one who is lost. (Luke 15)

God went after his lost son and daughter in the garden as soon as they sinned. (Gen.3:8-9) His question to them, "Where are you?" was not just a question about their location. God knew where the were, but did they? Their shame caused them to go into hiding. In one way or another, that is our story too. It's what stops us from being truly authentic.

Authenticity with self means admitting where you are without shame or hiding, but realizing that *where* you are is not *who* you are. Where you are, where you have been, or what you have done does not define who you are. The fact you have sinned doesn't mean your identity is framed in terms of your being a sinner. You are who and what God says you are.

When God created man and woman, he said his creation was very good. That is still true. You are immeasurably valuable to God. Your sin doesn't change that. After all, it was sinners for whom Christ came and died. Every person, whether or not a Christian, has incredible value to God.

However, if you put your faith in Christ, there's even better news: because of Jesus' life. death and ressurection you have been given a new, permanent identity. You now are a son or daughter of God himself, adopted into his eternal family. (Gal. 4:5-7) You are a joint heir with Christ entitled to all the riches Jesus enjoys as God's beloved Son. This means that when God looks at you, he doesn't see your past or your sin; he sees only Jesus. And whether or not you feel like one, the New Testament says that since you are "in Christ" you are a saint, a person declared holy by God.

Your new identity in Christ, however, has nothing to do with how you have performed (i.e, what you have done or not done). Instead, it has everything to do with what Christ has done for you and to whom you now belong. You are now God's beloved child. He loves you not for what you have done but for who you are. You are his child. Get that through your head and into your heart. You belong to God. He loves you as his own son or daughter. You are incredibly valuable to him, and when he looks at you, he sees the spitting image of his son Jesus.

So authenticity means you can be open about where you have been and what you have done, because you are confident about whose you are. You have nothing to prove and nothing to lose. This is the most freeing position in all the world!

When you finally understand that there is nothing that you or anyone else can do or say about you that can change your identity or your value, you are free! You can stop hiding, pretending or trying to impress those around you and recognize that you now are free to live for an audience of one. When your identity is that of a child of God, you can look honestly at your weaknesses and failures and confess them openly without fear of judgement or condemnation on God's part. What a re-lief that is! No pretending. No proving. This really is the starting point for everything good in your life.

Where you are is not who you are.
Whose you are makes you who you are.
You are God's child.

GROUP DISCUSSION QUESTIONS

1. What stood out to you in the reading?

2. What do you think makes it difficult for people to accept themselves where they are?

3. Where are you now in your relationship with God and your progress in becoming like Jesus?

4. Where would you like to be?

5. How does knowing who you are make it easier to be honest about where you are?

WEEK 1 **DAILY DEVOTIONS**

DAY ONE
WHY WE HIDE

Where are you? That was the first question God asked in the Bible. He came to meet with the man and woman in the garden as he always did in the cool of the day. But like small children ashamed of their poopy diaper, they were hiding. (Gen. 3:8-9)

"Where are you?" God asked. "I was afraid, because I was naked, so I hid" came the ashamed reply. That has been the story of every one of Adam's sons and daughters since. We are afraid. We feel exposed. Believing we will be rejected if we are truly known, we go into hiding.

The elaborate figleaf of your personality, accomplishments, clothes or whatever other face you put on is your attempt to hide your shame.

It doesn't need to be hidden. It needs to be healed. Notice that in the story of Adam and Eve, God provides a better covering to replace the fig leaves. Through Jesus' death on the cross, you no longer need to cover up your brokenness. Jesus' sacrifice on your behalf provides a permanent covering. When God looks at you, he sees only Jesus, not your brokenness, failures or sin.

Like many of us, you may still bear the scars and shame from what you've done or what has been done to you. However, that past doesn't define you. Once you're "in Christ, where you have been or what you have done no longer defines you. God alone defines who you are, and he thinks you're wonderful. Who do you think you are?

What are some of the "fig leaves" you have hid behind? Write a prayer confessing them to God.

<hr />

NOTES

SINNERS AND SAINTS

When you become a Christian, you are no longer a sinner. Your old self died with Jesus, and you have been reborn just as surely as Jesus has been raised from the dead. You are a new creation and now carry the nature of Christ instead of Adam. If you doubt this, read Romans 5-6!

You may wonder, "Then why do I still sin if I'm not a sinner?" Good question! I'm glad you asked. You sin because you choose to. Adam and Eve were created without sin but with a free will. They didn't have a sinful nature. They didn't have to sin, but they still chose to sin. And they did it on behalf of the whole human family.

As their descendant, you may have been born a sinner, but when you became a Christian, you died with Christ. (Rom. 6:4) You are no longer someone who can't "not sin". You now have the same free state of choice in which Adam and Eve started. (Rom 6:7) But even though you are no longer a sinner and can choose not to sin, you can also still choose to sin. (Rom. 6:11-13)

Jesus was subject to temptation and could have chosen to sin. But he chose not to. Temptation came to Jesus. It was real. But his nature was not predisposed to evil, and he didn't let it trip him up. You have his nature now, and you no longer need to be tripped up by the temptations to sin that you face either.

The problem is that you have chosen sin enough times in your life that you have created habits of thinking, feeling and acting that are sinful. These habits are simply pathways in your brain that automate behavior that you can change with practice. They are your habits, but they are not your nature.

As a Christian, your new nature is to be like God. That was the original design (Gen. 1:26) and the pre planned destiny for which you were redeemed! (Romans 8:29) Believing your nature is sinful keeps you stuck and hopeless, waiting for death to save you from yourself instead of understanding that you are already saved by Jesus!

You have an enemy who loves to lie to you and tell you that you are a sinner . . . that you like sin . . . that God is not enough for you . . . that you deserve it . . . etc. And you sometimes fall for those lies because they seem true at the time. But when you recognize them as lies and you understand their source, you don't have to fall for them.

When you go around confusing your habits or your thoughts with your nature, you end up fighting yourself, hating yourself and punishing yourself. Guess whose agenda that serves!

Spend some time journaling about some of the ways that believing you are a sinner keeps you stuck in sin. How does understanding your nature as created and recreated in the image of God empower you to change?

NOTES

NOTES

NOTES

DAY THREE
A GOOD TREE BEARS GOOD FRUIT

Jesus says that "every good tree bears good fruit." (Matthew 7:17). In Jesus' analogy, a person is the tree and the fruit are the things that bloom from that person (actions, words, accomplishments, etc.). This truth at times is difficult to accept. You may sometimes ask yourself, "What if I find myself doing bad things and bad fruit grows from my life? Does that mean I am not a good tree?"

In response to this question, you might frantically try to attach good fruit to your branches to prove that you are one of the good trees Jesus is talking about. You then feel despair when the good fruit won't stick to the branches. That is because you are starting in the wrong place. You are trying to deal with the fruit in hopes that it will transform the tree. You are trying to deal with your outward actions in hopes that it will transform your heart.

Imagine how foolish (and unsuccessful) a farmer would be if he tried to operate this way. You'd tell him, "If you want healthy fruit you need a healthy tree!" In the same way, you need God's Spirit to transform your heart if good fruit is to grow naturally from your life. It's a process of accepting who God has created you to be (a good tree) and who he has already declared you to be in Christ (a saint, not a sinner). When you open your heart to the identity that you have "in Christ" and allow his transformative power to nurture your heart back to health, the good fruit will grow from there.

Talk to God about where you have trouble accepting your identity as a "good tree" in Christ. Ask him what he wants you to believe about yourself. Journal what you sense he might be saying in the space provided.

NOTES

TENDING THE SOIL

Yesterday we talked about how accepting in our hearts our identity as saints allows the corresponding fruit to grow naturally from that identity. But what does this process look like? What does it mean to accept our true identity as a child of God? Looking closer at Jesus' word picture may help us to understand better.

Jesus says "every good tree bears good fruit, but a bad tree bears bad fruit." (Matthew 7:17) The principle is simple: a healthy tree will produce healthy fruit, while an unhealthy tree will produce unhealthy fruit or no fruit at all. So what does it take to make a tree healthy? Those of you with a green thumb know that it means making sure the plant has all that it needs: water, proper sunlight, and fertile soil. You have to put the plant in the best possible position to succeed and then let mother nature do her thing.

So what does it take to make the tree of your heart spiritually healthy? How can you put it in the best possible position to bear good fruit? There are helpful spiritual practices (spiritual disciplines) that can help you tend the soil of your heart. (See page 143)

These practices are not transformative in and of themselves. As Paul reminds us, "neither the one who plants nor the one who waters is anything, but only God, who makes things grow." (1 Corinthians 3:7). Though these practices are helpful in tending to the soil of your heart, God's power in Christ is what transforms you. So don't look at these practices as a checklist of things to do in order to please God. That was the Pharisees' mistake. Think of them instead as tools to prepare your heart for God's transforming power.

You will need to clear out the rocks of sin from the soil, and the weeds that crowd out God's best. You'll need to guard against the birds that want to steal from you and make sure you get exposure to the light of God's presence and the water of his Spirit. (Mark 4)

Get outside and meditate on how things grow. Write down your thoughts below.

NOTES

DON'T MISS THE POINT

On a particular Sabbath day, Jesus and his disciples were walking in a grainfield and started to get hungry. His disciples stopped and picked up some of the heads of grain that had fallen to the ground. The Pharisees were outraged, "Look, why are they doing what is unlawful on the Sabbath?" (Mark 2:24) Jesus' response shows that the Pharisees were missing the point entirely. He said, "The Sabbath was made for man, not man for the Sabbath." (Mark 2:27)

The Pharisees had a fatal misconception of the purpose of the Sabbath. They believed that they needed to observe the commandments perfectly in order to please God. Jesus turns this idea on its head. He points out that, in fact, the Sabbath was created by God to serve your needs! Setting aside a day of rest each week is a worthwhile practice (spiritual discipline) that can build a healthy rhythm of connection with God and restoration into your life. Like all spiritual disciplines, it is a tool, not a rule.

You can make religious systems, traditions, and spiritual disciplines your focus in hopes that your adherence to them will please God. What if you asked instead, "What practices best open my heart to God and reinforcing my true identity in Christ?" When you understand what Jesus has already done for you, it helps these practices fall into their proper place. Then you are free to find the practices that are most helpful for you.

Look through the list of disciplines in the Extras Section in the back of the book. Pick one that you believe can serve you and give it a try this week. Rememeber, the disciplines aren't the point, but they can help you be open to God.

WEEK 2 **GETTING BETTER**

Though God meets us where we are, he is not content to leave us there. Because we are his kids, he wants us to grow up to be the spitting image of our Father. God's plan was always for Jesus to be the firstborn of many brothers and sisters. He wants us to grow up into all his fullness and to live into the glory he planned for us all along — our pre-planned destiny to be like Jesus.

So he works with everything (the good and bad we do and everything that happens to us) to make us more like Jesus. He makes it all work together for good in the end (Romans 8:28). So if it's not good, it's not the end! This doesn't mean that God causes everything in our lives. It means that no matter what happens, God can work it out for our good. And he will. Always.

In the middle of it, sometimes it doesn't look like God is doing anything. Think of the story of Joseph that takes up the second half of Genesis. As a teenager, Joseph dreamed of God's special destiny for him, but then he got thrown into a pit, sold into slavery, falsely accused, thrown into prison and forgotten in prison by the people he had helped get out! He probably didn't "feel God's guiding hand" in the middle of all that. But God was with him. God was working it together for Joseph's good.

By the end of the story, Joseph faces the brothers who betrayed him. He realizes that though his brothers' actions were evil and entirely their fault, God worked them together for good. God used the chain of events to bring about not only Joseph's good, but the good of the people of Egypt and Israel! Nothing can mess up

God's plan. The suffering in the middle of our stories can serve as a catalyst for growth. It creates an opportunity for our redeeming God to do what he does best!

Think about your own life story and step back to see how God is working all things together for your good and as a blessing to others. It might help you to share your story with others. Sometimes others can spot God's mysterious work even when you can't. The following exercise can help you map out and share your story.

GROUP EXPERIENCE:
STORYBOARD

This activity is intended to help you practice being authentic with yourself, God, and others, looking at both the good and the bad.

Materials:
- Blank sheet of paper (one per person)
- Pen or pencil
- Crayons and/or colored pencils (optional)

Instructions:
1. Using your entire paper, create six even sections. Take 10 minutes to draw six sketches representing the moments, people, or things that have most shaped your life up to today.

2. When you have finished, spend a few minutes talking to Jesus about each sketch, what it represents, and how you feel about it. Ask him if he has anything to say about what you've drawn.

3. Take turns having each person share their storyboard, describing what they drew and why they drew it. After

each person has finished sharing give a minute or two for others to ask the sharer follow up questions about his or her sketches and offer encouragement. Conclude each sharer's time by having one person lead the group in a brief prayer for the sharer.

4. If your group is larger than 8 people you may consider splitting your group in half to assure you have enough time for everyone to share. If you do split in half, come back together and spend some time discussing what the experience of sharing was like.

REMINDERS:

* These sketches can represent good or bad times. All of our lives have both.

* This is about telling your story authentically, not about being a good artist. You are free to be as creative or not creative as you'd like.

* Words are welcome but use them sparingly. No need to write your story out.

* If you get stuck, jot down a list of events or time periods that you might want to include on the back of your page and then narrow it down to the six most important.

* Use this as a prayerful time between you and God, as you reflect on your life together.

WEEK 2 **DAILY DEVOTIONS**

DAY ONE

PLOTLINE OF MY LIFE

Living authentically isn't easy, especially when taking into account your story. Though you've had amazing moments in your life, you've also had moments of sadness, shame, and pain. These moments are sometimes difficult to understand, especially considering that Romans 8:28 tells us that "in all things God works for the good of those who love him, who have been called according to his purpose."

Now notice that it does not say "God causes all things and then works them for the good." God never causes evil or wishes evil to befall those he loves. Rather, he redeems what was intended for evil for the good. In light of some of your life stories, that may not seem right and can leave you with questions.

Talk to God about what stands out to you in Romans 8:28. What about this truth brings you hope? Is there anything about this truth that is difficult for you? Be open with God about how you feel.

NOTES

NOTES

DAY TWO
DEVELOPING CHARACTERS

Characters in a story develop through suffering, loss and struggle. You know this intuitively as you read stories and watch movies. If Rocky was always on top from the beginning and never lost or struggled, his story would be boring. When Frodo Baggins finally destroys the ring of power, you feel the strength of character it took because you have watched his struggle for so many pages of the story or hours on screen. Suffering and growth are intertwined. Even Jesus grew through suffering:

> *Son though he was, he learned obedience from what he suffered and, once made perfect, he became the source of eternal salvation for all who obey him. Heb. 5:8*

The character of everyone is developed through suffering and struggle. Of course you would rather grow without suffering. But it doesn't work that way. Your struggle and the hard parts of your story help make you who you are. They teach you lessons you couldn't have learned any other way. They develop endurance and perseverance and faith.

The sooner you recognize this universal truth and embrace it, the sooner you can get on with being conformed to the image of Jesus.

What are some lessons you have learned through your suffering? What are some ways your character has been shaped through struggle?

NOTES

HEART MATTERS

Your heart matters to God. It always has and always will. His intention for you since the beginning of creation was a full and abundant life:

> *The thief comes only to steal and kill and destroy; I have come that they may have life, and have it to the full. John 10:10*

Based on that verse you can see that your heart really matters. It matters so much that there is an enemy, a thief, dead-set against it. His only aim is to shut it down and destroy it. His aim is to steal, kill and destroy the full abundant life God intends for you. Andy Stanley has observed that:

> *"Life can be hard on the heart. The world is full of outside influences that have the power to disrupt the rhythm of your heart . . . over time you develop habits that slowly erode your heart's sensitivity. The inevitable pain and disappointment of life can cause you to set up walls around your heart . . . YOUR HEART IS OUT OF SYNC WITH THE RHYTHM IT WAS CREATED TO MAINTAIN."*

Think back to the very first time your heart was broken. Briefly identify and write what happened, how you felt and how it began to change you or your perspective. Now write about what were you like BEFORE that happened.

Write a prayer as a way to bring that heartbreak to God. You may want to read some of the Psalms as David expressed similar prayers. If you find one that speaks for you, feel free to use and personalize it.

NOTES

DAY FOUR
ENCOURAGING YOURSELF

One of the greatest things someone said to my wife Traci along her healing journey was, "YOU MADE IT!"

That struck her so deeply because she never really thought about it before; She never truly acknowledged her life as a victory at that point. This person also asked her to imagine herself as a young girl, before her heart was broken by the world for the first time, and to tell her younger self that she was gonna make it. Not only was she gonna make it but she was gonna be INCREDI-BLE!

This led her to write a letter to that little girl Traci and encourage her about what's to come. She gave her younger self all the bits of wisdom and advice the older Traci had learned over the years. It was so healing and good for her heart. Why don't you try it?

Write a letter to the younger you and let him or her know that no matter what happens, "YOU'RE GONNA MAKE IT!"

Traci's letter is below, for you to see an example.

> *Hi Traci,*
>
> *You don't know me yet, but I'm the older you. I know you can't even imagine that you're gonna be me in 43 years but trust me, it's true.*
>
> *First, I just wanna say you're my favorite person on the planet. You're seriously the cutest lil thing. I love how your sense of joy is*

contagious. You make everyone around you happy and can create fun in every situation. Second, I love your sense of imagination. You are creative and create fun and interesting scenarios to play for hours. Your friends really like that too. Everyone wants to be around you because of it!

Finally, you bring all that to your family, especially your brothers. You have no idea how important that will be in the years to come and what they'll remember about you.

I'm just writing to you to remind you of these things because (don't freak out) some hard times are gonna come. But you're not alone. EVERYONE goes through difficulties in life. I promise, you won't be the only one.

I also wanted to tell you that even more important than knowing others are going through hard times too; what's even MORE important is that you realize that Jesus, though you can't see him, is literally with you every step of the way. You can use that great imagination of yours and picture Jesus as a good, loving and strong daddy -- holding you when you're sad, fighting the bad guys when they're mean to you, cheering you on when you feel like you can't do it, and reminding you of your strength and how smart you are when you forget.

Though we live in a big, beautiful, fun world, I want you to also know that people get to make their own choices and sometimes they make bad ones. But Jesus will be your best friend and will help you know what to do, how to handle it, and get through it as an even stronger, smarter girl than you were before.

You're a fighter Traci. Did I tell you that? It's partly because you are growing up with so many tough boys in your family, but it's mostly because that's how God made you. You are a fighter not because you're angry but because you will begin to see how to have victory in the trials that come your way. And you're gonna eventually teach others how to do the same when you're my age. I don't want to spoil the surprise, but just keep learning all the important things that made you who you are. Because when you're my age you'll use all that information in your favorite job of all time! (Don't ask me what job that is cuz I'm not gonna tell you. You'll just have to see when you get there!)

Anyway Trace, you got this! You're gonna be a rockstar in this thing called life! I'm excited for you to experience all there is. Remember this letter. Take it out every once in a while and read it. It's gonna help you, I promise!

Love you sweetheart,

Traci

NOTES

PRINCIPLES OF INNER HEALING

Jesus came to heal the brokenhearted and set the captives free physically and spiritually.

> *The Spirit of the Sovereign Lord is upon me. He has anointed me to preach good news to the poor. He has sent me to bind up the brokenhearted, to proclaim freedom for the captives and release from darkness for the prisoners. (Isaiah 61:1)*

Isaiah 61 was not only Jesus' mission to establish the kingdom on earth as it is in heaven, but it's our mission too. Jesus cares how people are doing on the inside. Broken hearts needs healing. Those captive to sin need freeing. We all need more freedom and light.

Rusty Rustenbach breaks down five principles of inner healing in his book, A Guide For Listening and Inner Healing Prayer (p.32-37)

Review each of Rustenbach's five principles below and journal about the questions.

Principle 1 - All of us have had our hearts broken.

Are you aware of ways in which yours may be broken or has been broken?

Principle 2 - The heart broke in response to something in the past.

This is about how your heart was shattered by one or more events that took place while you were growing up. **Ask God to reveal one or two instances when your heart may have been broken. What does he bring to mind?**

Principle 3 - Our reaction to events, not events themselves, place us in bondage.

This clarifies that our captivity doesn't come from how badly we were hurt. It comes from what we came to believe as a result of the event. **Which of the sources of woundedness seems to best describe how you were hurt (self wounding, wounded by someone else, sin in reaction to hurt, or a misinterpretation of a neutral event)?**

If someone else hurt you, was it active abuse (something the person did), passive abuse (something the person neglected to do), or a mixture of both?

Principle 4 - Present difficulties often trigger past pain.

Ask God about this: "Jesus, in the last week or month, did something disagreeable happen in my interactions with others where I may have overreacted?"

Principle 5 - Life changing truth can be known and experienced when God communicates it to us in a supernatural way

This is about the importance of God supernaturally communicating his life changing truth to us. **Is there a time when you were influenced by a communication from God. If so, describe that time and what you learned.**

NOTES

WITH GOD

WEEK 3 **STAYING CONNECTED**

You and I were made by a relational God for a relational God. Out of the loving intimacy they shared within the Trinity, the Father, Son and Holy Spirit chose to expand the family and create humans to share in the abundance of this intimate relationship and family resemblance.

You were created for intimacy with God. The only way you will experience the abundant life you want is to stay connected to him. Sustaining that connection is the key to everything good in life. Jesus creates that connection, but whether that connection is sustained is up to you. God allows you to freely choose how you respond to him. He will not force himself on you. He is a gentleman.

Four times on the night before he was crucified, Jesus

told his disciples that God would answer their prayers. He told them to "ask for whatever you want, and it will be as good as done." However, he set one condition to receiving the benefits of that incredible promise: that you "remain in him".

You remain or abide in Jesus like a branch that is connected to a vine. You don't create the connection. It exists. Humanity was originally created in that connection. Jesus redeemed that connection when it was broken by sin. Now that we have been reconnected to God we just have to stay connected to him. Remain in him.

But how exactly do we do that? Let's look at what Jesus said about this in more detail.

The five sections below (Believe, Ask, Love, Identify, and Unite) outline what remaining in intimacy with God looks like according to Jesus. Read each section and then discuss the corresponding question that follows before moving on to the next section.

BELIEVE

*Philip said, "Lord, show us the Father and that will be enough for us." Jesus answered: "Don't you know me, Philip, even after I have been among you such a long time? Anyone who has seen me has seen the Father. How can you say, 'Show us the Father'? Don't you believe that I am in the Father, and that the Father is in me? The words I say to you I do not speak on my own authority. Rather, it is the Father, living in me, who is doing his work. Believe me when I say that I am in the Father and the Father is in me; or at least believe on the evidence of the works themselves. Very truly I tell you, whoever believes in me will do the works I have been doing, and they will do even greater things than these, because I am going to the Father. And I will do whatever you ask in my name, so that the Father may be glorified in the Son. **You may ask me for*** *anything in my name, and I will do it." (John 14:8–14)*

Our starting point for truly knowing God is *believing that Jesus is how we see who God is.* The Bible tells us that Jesus, the Son, is the perfect picture of what God the Father is like. If you have seen Jesus, you have seen God. God, who is invisible became visible in the person of Jesus. The Jesus you read about in the New Testament is what God is truly like. There is no other way to see or know God as he truly is. Get to know Jesus and you will get to know God.

Discuss: How does your view of what God is like affect your ability to connect with him?

ASK

*"Remain in me, as I also remain in you. No branch can bear fruit by itself; it must remain in the vine. Neither can you bear fruit unless you remain in me. I am the vine; you are the branches. If you remain in me and I in you, you will bear much fruit; apart from me you can do nothing. If you do not remain in me, you are like a branch that is thrown away and withers; such branches are picked up, thrown into the fire and burned. If you remain in me and my words remain in you, **ask whatever you wish, and it will be done for you.** This is to my Father's glory, that you bear much fruit, showing yourselves to be my disciples." (John 15:4–8)*

Even if you believe that Jesus shows us what God is like, you must remain connected to Jesus to bear any fruit (i.e. for your life to produce love, joy, peace, patience, kindness, goodness, faithfulness, gentleness and self-control).

Prayer is an essential element of remaining connected to God. It connects our heart to his. Prayer is simply talking to God about anything and everything. Simply express your desires, needs, frustrations, dreams, joys and heartaches to God in your own words at any time throughout your day. Thank him for who he is and what he has done for you, and share with him things you wouldn't feel comfortable sharing with anyone else.

Asking is one part of prayer; essential to receiving what God wants to give you. Jesus said people often don't receive what they want and need because they don't ask. While God is not your personal genie, he is a loving Father who delights in giving good gifts to his children. He will respond to your prayer by doing what's best for you. That answer may be "yes', "no" or "not now". He may even answer your request with something much better than you even asked for.

But this asking is essential to developing intimacy. It's how children bond to their parents through having their needs met. With God also, we learn to ask for what we need and want and to trust our heavenly Father whether the answer is yes, no or not now. As we grow in our knowledge of God's ways, we learn to ask things in line with his will. Our will begins to be conformed to his as we mature.

The give and take of the relationship creates more intimacy. You ask. God answers. You respond in gratitude. Your life begins bearing fruit. That fruitfulness gives God glory and gives you joy. It's a beautiful cycle that flows out of relationship. It's not magic. It's intimacy.

Discuss: How does making requests lead to more intimacy? What kind of asking doesn't lead to intimacy?

LOVE

*As the Father has loved me, so have I loved you. Now remain in my love. If you keep my commands, you will remain in my love, just as I have kept my Father's commands and remain in his love. I have told you this so that my joy may be in you and that your joy may be complete. My command is this: love each other as I have loved you. Greater love has no one than this: to lay down one's life for one's friends. You are my friends if you do what I command. I no longer call you servants, because a servant does not know his master's business. Instead, I have called you friends, for everything that I learned from my Father I have made known to you. You did not choose me, but I chose you and appointed you so that you might go and bear fruit—fruit that will last—and **so that whatever you ask in my name the Father will give you**. This is my command: Love each other." (John 15:9–17)*

When we obey God it strengthens our connection to him. Jesus said that all God's commandments to us could be summarized as follows: "Love God and love others." When we love those God loves, we are loving God. In laying down our lives for each other, we are not only imitating Jesus, we are showing that we care about what he cares about. We are his friends. So he shares more of his heart with us and our intimacy with him deepens. We are invited beyond being servants into the realm of family.

Discuss: Who has loved you in a sacrificial way? Can you give an example?

IDENTIFY

*"In that day you will no longer ask me anything. Very truly I tell you, **my Father will give you whatever you ask in my name**. Until now you have not asked for anything in my name. **Ask and you will receive, and your joy will be complete**. Though I have been speaking figuratively, a time is coming when I will no longer use this kind of language but will tell you plainly about my Father.*

In that day you will ask in my name. I am not saying that I will ask the Father on your behalf. No, the Father himself loves you because you have loved me and have believed that I came from God. I came from the Father and entered the world; now I am leaving the world and going back to the Father." (John 16:23–28)

Jesus gives us direct access to God the Father. You don't need another mediator between you and God. As you stay connected to Jesus in intimacy, you learn to love what he loves and want what he wants. Then he can trust us with his own "all-access pass" to the Father! That's what asking in Jesus' "name" means. He allows us to "drop his name." He lets us charge things to his account!

When we identify our lives with Jesus this way and approach the Father as if we were the beloved Son in whom he is well pleased, we have stepped into a new level of intimacy with the Father and the Son. You could even say, we have stepped into the intimacy of the Father and the Son AS the Son.

Discuss: What is exciting about identifying with Jesus and asking "in his name"? How can asking "in Jesus' name" (or using his bank card) change how you live?

UNITE

*"My prayer is not for them alone. I pray also for those who will believe in me through their message, that all of them may be **one, Father, just as you are in me and I am in you. May they also be in us** so that the world may believe that you have sent me. I have given them the glory that you gave me, that they may be one as we are one—I in them and you in me—so that they may be brought to **complete unity. Then the world will know that you sent me and have loved them even as you have loved me."** (John 17:20–23)*

In the previous passage, the profound intimacy with God you have available through Jesus culminates in this amazing idea. You share in the oneness of the Trinity. Your invitation is not to worship from a distance, but to marry into the family as part of the one bride of Christ. This spiritually unites all believers in a way that transcends our differences if we will let it. And it has the power to make the world take notice.

It is an unimaginable mystery how a husband and wife become one. Paul says it is the same way with the Messiah and the Church. (Eph. 5:31-32) We are invited into the very heart of the Trinity. The Father, Son and Spirit are not a closed circle. They have forever opened the circle to us! Now the eternal, abundant, life-giving God has invited us into that circle of joy and love and peace forever.

Discuss: How does this idea of being invited into the life and relationship of the Trinity feel to you? How could your life be different if you really believed you had this much access to God?

GROUP DISCUSSION

Discuss the reading as a whole. What about this idea stands out to you? What is confusing? Which of these five actions do you most need to take to nurture your connection to God?

WEEK 3 **DAILY DEVOTIONS**

DAY ONE
YOUR HOME IN JESUS

> *I am the vine; you are the branches. If you remain in me and I in you, you will bear much fruit; apart from me you can do nothing. (John 15:5)*

Jesus' illustration is simple: in the same way a branch needs to be connected to a vine or a tree to grow and bear fruit, you need to be connected to Jesus to grow spiritually and bear spiritual character similar to his. A vine is the life source for a branch. It is responsible for collecting and providing all the nutrients and water that the branch needs in order to grow. The branch's job is simply to receive. But Jesus is clear that the branch must be open to receiving from the vine. The vine will not force the branch; the branch must "remain."

In other translations, the word "remain" is translated "abide," the same root word as "abode" *aka* "home." Jesus in a very real sense is saying, "make your home in me. Get comfortable. Kick your feet up. Stay a while." Jesus' invitation to remain is one of peace and refuge, rest and relationship. But he won't force this home upon you. If you want to enjoy it and all the life that flows from it, you have to choose it for yourself. It is the home your soul was made to dwell in.

Spend some time making your home in Jesus and in his love. That may mean spending five minutes just sitting with him or some time unpacking all that is

on your mind with him by journalling or speaking out loud to Jesus. Do whatever makes you feel most at home with him today.

NOTES

INVITED INTO THE FAMILY

God decided in advance to adopt us into his own family by bring-
ing us to himself through Jesus Christ. This is what he wanted to
do, and it gave him great pleasure.(Ephesians 1:5)

You were never an afterthought to God. From the beginning, you were adopted in the beloved Son of God.
His intention was always to adopt you and me into his
family.

What family? We aren't talking about Abraham's family
or even the idea of the church as a family. No, it is *God's*
family. The eternal Trinity created you for fellowship as
a member of God's family!

Read through Ephesians 1:3-15 and write your own
paraphrase of it, personalizing it by changing the plu-
rals to singular. Us becomes me. We becomes I.

NOTES

NOTES

MY SHEEP HEAR MY VOICE

My sheep hear my voice, and I know them, and they follow me.
(John 10:27)

The LORD is my shepherd, and his name is Jesus. Jesus
takes the good shepherd imagery of the Psalms and
prophets and declares that he is the good shepherd.
In the book of Ezekiel, God had promised to come in
person to shepherd his sheep and here he was! (Ezekiel.
34:15)

Do you know that like sheep, you were created to hear
and respond to the voice of your shepherd Jesus? It
doesn't require any special skill, just your attention. The
more you listen to him the more you will recognize his
voice. But first you have to believe he is speaking to
you.

God rarely speaks out loud in an audible voice. He
speaks from deep within your heart. Tune in and listen
to him from there. His voice may be faint at first, but
the more you practice, the clearer it will become.

**Ask God what he is doing in your life and relationship
with him right now. Spend some time listening to how
he responds, paying attention to life-giving things
that are impressed on your heart and come to your
mind. Journal about your experience.**

NOTES

GETTING CLOSER

Until you are filled to the complete measure of the fullness of God the way Jesus was, you have only scratched the surface of what is possible for you to experience in intimate relationship with God. Read this passage together with the Holy Spirit in dialog with the Father and the Son. Meditate on it and ask questions that come to mind. See what stands out to you and let it be a jumping off point for you to get to know the God who loves you and wants to fill you completely with himself!

> *For this reason I kneel before the Father, from whom every family in heaven and on earth derives its name. I pray that out of his glorious riches he may strengthen you with power through his Spirit in your inner being, so that Christ may dwell in your hearts through faith. And I pray that you, being rooted and established in love, may have power, together with all the Lord's holy people, to grasp how wide and long and high and deep is the love of Christ, and to know this love that surpasses knowledge—that you may be filled to the measure of all the fullness of God. (Eph. 3:14-19)*

NOTES

NOTES

DAY FIVE

A LIFE WALKING WITH GOD

But the fruit of the Spirit is love, joy, peace, forbearance, kindness, goodness, faithfulness, gentleness and self-control. Against such things there is no law. Those who belong to Christ Jesus have crucified the flesh with its passions and desires. Since we live by the Spirit, let us keep in step with the Spirit. (Galatians 5:22-25)

Have you ever been on a walk with someone and realized that your stride had paced itself to theirs? What if this somewhat weird phenomenon was true with our walk with God as well? What if, as you walked more with him, you started to walk more like him? This is exactly the picture that is painted in the passage above. As we walk with God's Spirit our stride will start to match his and the fruit of the Spirit will begin to grow naturally from our lives.

The point of this passage isn't to grit your teeth and have more self control or to bring about a more faith-filled life through sheer force of will. The fruit of God's Spirit is not something you can force. It is a byproduct of your connection and journeying with him.

As you join him in this journey and practice a life of continual conversation and connection, you will start to gain a sensitivity to the gentle push and pull of his Spirit. It is almost like developing a sixth sense for how God's Spirit is moving in each moment of your life; to the point that you may at times even unconsciously follow his lead.

What would it look like for you to walk more in step with God's Spirit today? Try to be more conscious of the movement of God's Spirit throughout your day.

You can even put a hair tie around your wrist or a sticky note on the back of your phone to remind you. Every time you become aware of this reminder say a short prayer simply asking "Lord what are you up to?" At the end of your day journal about the experience.

NOTES

WEEK 4 **GETTING CLOSER**

In the following group experience listen as the imaginative prayer is being read aloud to the entire group. As you listen, pay attention to your imagination and the visuals God is bringing to mind. At each pause (marked by a gap in the text), write down what you see. If you are facilitating the reading, be sure to enter into the experience yourself, making the most of the pauses. Each pause should be 20-30 seconds at least. Use this as a time to connect with God through the creativity of the imagination he has given you.

IMAGINATIVE PRAYER
JESUS' GIFT

Imagine yourself in a beautiful area of nature that you've been before. What does it look like?... What do you see?... What do you smell?... How do you feel?

You find yourself walking through the beauty, enjoying the moment, and you see a water feature. It completes the scene you are looking at just perfectly. What is it?

As you explore, you look down and realize you are on a path. So you continue along peacefully. You look into the distance and you see a figure in front of you, but you don't know who it is. You feel safe enough to walk up to the figure, and you discover it's Jesus. What is he wearing? What does he look like? What do you sense about him?

You sit somewhere with him. Where is it? How do you feel?

He reaches behind his back and pulls out a gift. He hands it to you. What does it look like? What are your thoughts?

You open the gift. What is it?

What did Jesus give you and only you? Ask him why he gave you that particular gift. What does he say?

You say your goodbyes, but it's not really a farewell, but more of a "see you later". You watch as Jesus walks one way and you walk the other as you carry your gift closely to your heart.

Write down any additional thoughts about your imaginative prayer experience. Be prepared to share with the group.

NOTES

WEEK 4 **DAILY DEVOTIONS**

DAY ONE
SILENCE AND SOLITUDE

Jesus often withdrew to lonely places and prayed. (Luke 5:16)

Silence is one of the easiest ways to open up your heart to God. Spend five minutes or more sitting with God in silence both externally and internally (you may want to set a timer). Take note of any thoughts or feelings that rise to the surface, but allow them to just float on by, returning to your silent state. Remember, this isn't about being good at it or achieving anything. Simply be with God.

Once your time is up, spend some time journaling to God about the experience.

NOTES

NOTES

DAY TWO
CAST YOUR CARES

Read 1 Peter 5:7

> *"Cast all your anxieties on him because he cares for you."*

Sometimes you feel alone in the worries and stresses of your life. You are never alone. God is with you and he cares for you. He wants to carry your burdens with you. What is weighing down your heart today? Will you give it to him?

Below, draw a large heart. Spend 10 minutes drawing where your heart is today as an act of prayer, presenting all of it to the Lord. Give him the anxiety weighing it down.

NOTES

NOTES

DAY THREE
BREATH PRAYER

Decide on a time and peaceful location where you
can be quiet. Anything from Bethel Music is a great
playlist for you to use if you prefer. If you listen to the
worship, use the phrase, "Abba, I belong to you" as
a breath prayer while you walk and/or listen. As you
breathe in, internally say, "Abba" and as you exhale
say, "I belong to you". Make this phrase a reality as
you continue to spend time with your heavenly Father.

Feel free to use any phrase from the worship songs
you listen to as a way to practice breath prayer.

NOTES

NOTES

DAY FOUR

WALKING

Jesus does a lot of walking in the gospels. It's a good thing too. Half of his life-altering encounters with people happened when he was walking by. Had he been in a car, he might have stopped for gas in Jericho, but he might never have met the nameless blind beggar or the famously short Zacchaeus.

Now we get to join him. That's why we walk around in our cities and our lives with our eyes wide open to the needs around us. Some are obvious. Others are not so apparent. But the Spirit of Jesus lives in us and helps us to see what he sees. Our part is just to take him for a walk and see what he wants to do! Because that same Spirit has the power to do more than we could imagine. **So go . . . walk with Jesus!**

NOTES

PSALMS

Read Psalm 139

The Psalms are different from other parts of the Bible in that they often reflect the personal prayers of the author. They contain many truths about who God is and who we are, while also revealing the messiness of where the author is in his life and walk with God. Reading this off-putting (and at times violent) messiness can make us uncomfortable (e.g. verses 19-22), but it provides for us a model of honesty for our own prayer lives.

Write your own Psalm as a prayer to God. Be sure to include the truth of who God is and who you are in light of him, while also being authentic to where you are at. You can also find a Psalm for someone you care about. Use it as a prayer for them, inserting their name where applicable.

NOTES

NOTES

Love

FOR EACH PERSON

WEEK 5 **LOVE SINCERELY**

"Love must be sincere. Hate what is evil; cling to what is good. Be devoted to one another in love. Honor one another above yourselves." (Romans 12:9-10)

When we talk about love as a core value, it can sound like just a nice sentiment or even a cliche'. That's why we're more specific and say "love for each person". We must see each person as created uniquely in the image of God and worthy to be loved and respected whether they know God or not. We are devoted to one another, and we honor and cling to the good we see in each other even when there are evil parts we hate.

To love sincerely, we must cling to the good without being in denial about the bad. This is more than theoretical. Rather than just giving assent to the idea that we should love all humanity, we must learn to love the one in front of us at any given moment. Honestly, it's much easier loving humanity-at-large than the particular human who just backed into your car at Albertsons.

Feeling or Choice?

So what does it look like to love the people around us? Some say it is a feeling. Some say it is a choice. Really, it is both. You can choose to love when you don't feel like it. You do this by loving actions that transcend feelings. But who wants to be loved out of discipline? We need the discipline to love when feelings fade, but if it is to be sincere and from the heart it has to be felt.

When you feel love for someone it's not hard to act lovingly toward them. Men in love will write poetry or do things that would feel like a burden at any other time. When a man loves a woman, as the song goes, she can do no wrong. It's even easy to forgive when you feel love for someone.

So what if you don't feel love for someone? How can you change your feelings? Sometimes doing loving actions will lead to loving feelings. Especially when you realize that you have access to a love and affection greater than your own!

Love is a Power

We aren't just commanded by God to be loving; we are also empowered by God to be loving. That changes everything! The blessing of the new covenant is that God promised to put his own Spirit in his people and compel them to live and love the way he does. He would give them his heart and his Spirit so that they would want to keep his commandments.

God's own Spirit who lives inside us as his people actually gives us his love to draw on! He loves people perfectly and with deep affection. You have him living in you. That means you have access to God's love for people if you will tap into it. This is the secret of loving people you may not even like. It is the power to forgive people who don't deserve it. God gives you his own love to do the job where yours falls far short. This is a game-changer!

When Edison learned to harness electricity, he changed the world. As a result, you now have a power that doesn't depend on you that enables you to do things you could never do otherwise. You heat with it, cook with it, light a room with it and charge your phones with it. It's always available, but you have to choose to plug into it or turn it on. While you wouldn't mistake it for a feeling, you will certainly feel it if you make a mistake with your wiring! Like electricity, love is a power bigger than you that you can choose to access.

So rather than merely a choice or a feeling, love is a superpower! You must choose to tap into it before you feel it. But when you do, God's Spirit in you enables supernatural loving. And there is no feeling in the world better than that!

GROUP DISCUSSION

1. What parts of the reading stood out to you? What made that part stand out?

2. Describe what it feels like to be in love. How is it easier to love when you feel it?

3. When have you chosen to love when you didn't feel like it? Did feelings follow? How is love more than

feelings?

4. What person or people do you love whom others may find difficult to love? What person or people are difficult for you to love?

5. How could tapping into God's feelings about someone help you to love them?

———

NOTES

WEEK 5 **DAILY DEVOTIONS**

DAY ONE

TO LOVE OTHERS IS TO LOVE GOD

Begin by reading Matthew 25:31-46

To love each person IS to love God. Our love for God is expressed through our love for people. This is why Jesus added "love your neighbor as yourself" to the command to love God (Mark 12:30-31). They are one and the same. Parents feel loved and respected when their kids treat each other well. My son cannot say he loves and respects his parents while disobeying them and being mean to his sister. Love for parents is expressed through obedience to the command to love those they love. In the same way, our love for God is manifest through our love for his kids. The Apostle John put it this way, "Whoever claims to love God yet hates a brother or sister is a liar. For whoever does not love their brother and sister, whom they have seen, cannot love God, whom they have not seen." God's love is seen when we love people.

Look for one person to love today in a practical way. Keep in mind that God takes personally your action of love towards that person, and he feels loved as a result!

NOTES

NOTES

DAY TWO
SEEING OTHERS HOW GOD SEES THEM

"So from now on we regard no one from a worldly point of view. Though we once regarded Christ in this way, we do so no longer. Therefore, if anyone is in Christ, the new creation has come: The old has gone, the new is here!" (2 Corinthians 5:16-17)

To see others how God sees is to see them in Christ as a new creation, even if they don't see themselves that way yet! We are to look at others through the lens of redemption, not counting their sins against them, but looking at their potential. In 1 Corinthians 13 we see that love doesn't keep a record of wrongs and it also hopes all things. When we see past a person's failures and flaws and look forward toward his or her potential as a new creation in Christ, we are seeing that person through the lens of love. As we see another person this way, we can start to speak out about what we observe and encourage people to live into who they were created to be.

Take thirty seconds to ask God to place someone on your heart. Ask him, "How do you see _____?" Listen for what he says. Now be bold and encourage that person today in what you see! You don't have to use language like "God told me" or anything like that. Simply say, "I wanted to encourage you today. You are _____ , or I see this in you, or I feel like you _____."

Remember, love never fails!

NOTES

DAY THREE
I APPRECIATE YOU

"My command is this: Love each other as I have loved you." (John 15:12)

To appreciate someone is to see that person's true value. Jesus practiced this kind of love constantly with those he encountered, especially those who were continually undervalued by the rest of the world: the sinner, the broken, the blind, the beggar.

Jesus' friend Peter was someone who continually stumbled his way through being a disciple. He was constantly misunderstanding what Jesus meant. He had many moments of mistaken theology and misguided passion. On the night Jesus was arrested, he even famously denied knowing Jesus at all. Despite all these missteps, Jesus never gave up on Peter. He saw value in Peter beyond his mistakes. Jesus truly appreciated him. And as a result, Peter grew to become the "Rock" that Jesus saw he could be and became one of the founding leaders of the Christian church.

When Jesus looks at someone he sees his or her unique value as God's image-bearer, regardless of how worthless that person has been made to feel. We can join in with Jesus' love by seeing this value in others and helping them see it in themselves.

Ask God to reveal three people in your life right now that he wants you to appreciate. Asking for God's help, write down three ways you appreciate (value) each of those people. Find time this week to tell each person on your list why you appreciate them.

NOTES

DAY FOUR
PROMISE AND REQUEST

Have you ever thought about what moves an idea, concept, or a relationship forward? What takes something that is stuck and releases it into motion?

The answer is a promise or a request.

However, whether we make a promise or a request to ourselves or to others, nothing moves forward until we make and KEEP our word. Jesus states it so simply in Matthew 5:37, "All you need to say is simply 'Yes' or 'No'; anything beyond this comes from the evil one." Jesus' desire is that we be a people of our word. As people made in his image, we must keep our promises.

Jesus knew this. In fact he IS the Word. He is God's promise made flesh. He did what he said and as a result he propelled into action God's rescue plan for humanity.

We have the honor of being a people of promise whose word is our bond. We represent Jesus well and responsibly when we value our word. This is also how we create forward motion in our relationships.

Practice being an image bearer. Make and keep a promise today. Then notice what it releases into motion.

NOTES

NOTES

DAY FIVE

FORGIVE US AS WE FORGIVE

*Bear with each other and forgive one another if any of you has
a grievance against someone. Forgive as the Lord forgave you.
(Colossians 3:13)*

Forgiving another person can be a difficult task, especially when we have been deeply hurt by that person.
Deep in our hearts we sometimes hold resentment
that we didn't even realize was there. To top it all off,
fear often gets involved too. We fear that to forgive
that person means that we must again make ourselves
vulnerable to them, putting ourselves at risk for future
hurt. That's because we often get confused about what
forgiveness is.

Forgiveness is a journey that we embark on with God,
regardless if the other person is involved or not. Forgiveness does not require you to trust, be open to,
or even have relationship with the person who has
wronged you. The person who has wronged you
doesn't even have to be present for forgiveness to take
place. Forgiveness simply says, "you no longer owe me
anything." No apology. No penance. Nothing.

Forgiveness sets those you forgive free from any debt
they owe you. And in lifting the burden of unforgiveness, you will find that you too have been set free.

**Ask God if there is anyone you need to forgive today.
Spend a few minutes listening to his response. If any
unforgiveness comes up, declare out loud before God
and yourself, "God, I fully release _____ of
any debt they owe me for _____." The
feelings may take time to follow, but the alignment of
your will with God's will for your life can start today.**

NOTES

WEEK 6 **LOVE APPROPRIATELY**

And now these three remain: faith, hope and love. But the greatest of these is love. Follow the way of love and eagerly desire gifts of the Spirit, especially prophecy. For anyone who speaks in a tongue does not speak to people but to God. Indeed, no one understands them; they utter mysteries by the Spirit. But the one who prophesies speaks to people for their strengthening, encouraging and comfort. Anyone who speaks in a tongue edifies themself, but the one who prophesies edifies the church. (1 Cor. 13:13-14:4)

Love is the most important thing in the world. But not everyone experiences it the same way. Some people feel loved by a hug or other physical touch. Others are more impacted by encouraging words. You may be one of those people who gives and receives love by giving gifts or doing acts of service or who shows love by giving quality time to someone. One size does not fit all. Learning to listen well and study the people you love will help you use an appropriate approach at the right time.

Whether words are your natural love-language or not, we all need to learn to express our love in words. The spiritual gift of prophecy is the ability to speak words inspired by God. If God lives in you and you are one with him in intimate connection, you will be able to see people through God's eyes and tell them what you see. You will see the best in them. You will see their gifts and strengths in a way that they may not be able to see. It is a great gift you can offer to someone to tell them how God feels about them.

The passage quoted above from 1 Corinthians is saying that while speaking in tongues can be great for developing your intimacy with God in your secret prayer time, prophecy is something you should value and desire even more. Tongues is the ability to speak or pray from your heart in the Spirit in an unknown language. Like speaking a secret language between you and a friend, this is fun for the two of you but it leaves others out and makes them feel uncomfortable when you do it around them. In contrast, prophecy is a great way to love others.

Prophecy is simply speaking God's heart about someone or some situation in order to strengthen, encourage or comfort others. It doesn't mean you are a fortune teller or that you are predicting future events. But it can influence future events by seeing what God sees and declaring it. If I see leadership potential in you and I tell you, especially at a time where you may not see that in yourself, you can be edified (strengthened) or encouraged by that. If you believe it, you may actually have confidence to lead and you may start to do it. In this way, I haven't predicted your future, but I have had a part in creating it by speaking forth what God is saying. This is a powerful way to love people. Tell them what you see!

You can also ask God for a message to deliver to another person. Remember that it must be strengthening, encouraging or comforting or it doesn't fit the description of New Testament prophecy. Telling someone that bad things are going to happen to them or pointing out the flaws and imperfections you see in them has no place in the life of a Christian. We only speak what is useful for building others up that it may benefit the hearer. (Eph. 4:29).

Try the group exercise to practice seeing the best in each other. Then learn more about love languages in your readings this next week. Practice loving each person in a way that he or she gets it. It's fun!

GROUP EXPERIENCE:
WHAT I SEE IN YOU

This activity is intended to help you practice loving one another through strengthening, encouraging, and comforting words.

Materials:
- Cardstock/Paper plates for each person
- Pens
- Scotch tape

Instructions:
Tape a sheet of cardstock/paper plate on the back of each person with their name on it.

Set a timer for 7 minutes or so and have everyone stand up (you may even consider playing some worship music in the background). As you all move around the room, have each person write a word or phrase on other's cardstock/plates that describes that person (e.g. BRAVE, STRONG, COMPASSIONATE, NURTURING MOTHER, WISE & INTELLIGENT, etc.). Be prayerful as you go, allowing the Holy Spirit to speak through you.

When everyone has finished, sit in a circle. Without reading it, each person should pass their cardstock/ plate to the person on their right.

Take turns having the person to the right read aloud the truths written about the person to the left. Address what you are saying to that person directly with identity statements (e.g. if "Brave" is written, say "Nancy, you are Brave").

As your paper is being read, recognize what you are thinking as these words are being spoken over you. Are you able to accept them?

After everyone has finished, return the papers to their owners, have each person circle the word on his or her cardstock/plate that was the most difficult to accept.

Have each person share which word was the most difficult to accept. Ask if whoever wrote that particular word or phrase would mind sharing why they blessed that person with that particular word. Allow others to confirm how they see that quality or characteristic in that person as well.

After a person has shared, ask that person to repeat the phrase, "I receive what you said about me and I accept that I am _____."

Once everyone has finished sharing spend some time discussing the experience and praying for one another.

WEEK 6 **DAILY DEVOTIONS**

Love Language Test
Start your week by taking this Love Language Test online.
Love Language Test http://www.5lovelanguages.com/

What love language did you score highest on and which did you score lowest on? Does this surprise you? Why or why not?

DAY ONE
ACTS OF SERVICE

Acts of service means doing things you know the other would like you to do. You seek to please them by serving them, to express your love by doing things they would like. These acts require thought, planning, time, effort and energy. If done with a positive spirit, they are indeed expressions of love.

How does God love in this way? How can you love in this way?

NOTES

DAY TWO
QUALITY TIME

"Quality time" means giving someone your undivided attention. It's not sitting on the couch watching television with them. Spending time that way means Netflix or HBO gets the attention — not the other person. Time is a precious commodity. We all have multiple demands on our time, yet each of us has the exact same hours in a day. You can make the most of those hours by committing some of them to your spouse or another loved one. If your primary love language is quality time, spending time together is most important.

How does God love in this way? How can you love in this way?

———

NOTES

PHYSICAL TOUCH

We have long known that physical touch is an essential way of communicating emotional love. Numerous research projects in the area of child development have made that conclusion: babies who are held, stroked and kissed develop a healthier emotional life than those who are left for long periods of time without physical contact.

For some individuals, physical touch is their primary love language. Without it, they feel unloved. With it, their emotional tank is filled, and they feel secure in the love of the other. Implicit love touches require little time but much thought, especially if physical touch is not your primary love language and if you did not grow up in a "touching family."

How does God love in this way? How can you love in this way?

NOTES

NOTES

GIFTS

A gift is something you can hold in your hand and say, "Look, you were thinking of me," or, "you remembered me." You must be thinking of someone to give him or her a gift. The gift itself is a symbol of that thought. It doesn't matter whether it costs money. What is important is that you thought of them. And it is not the thought implanted only in the mind that counts but the thought expressed in actually securing the gift and giving it as the expression of love.

How does God love in this way? How can you love in this way?

––––––––

NOTES

NOTES

WORDS OF AFFIRMATION; LOVE IN A LETTER

One way to express love emotionally is to use words that build someone up. King Solomon, author of some of the Old Testament's wisdom literature, wrote, "The tongue has the power of life and death" (Proverbs 18:21).

One of our deepest human needs is the need to feel appreciated. Words of affirmation meet that need in many individuals.

How does God love in this way? How can you love in this way?

Write a letter to someone who is important to you. Some things to consider would be:

- What you appreciate about them

- What your love language is

- How that impacts that particular relationship

- What you've noticed about how they have seemed to experience love best

- What you've seen that gives you that idea

- How you are going to intentionally practice loving them in their "language" and write tangible ways for them to understand.

Consider presenting the letter to them in a way they would feel loved. (Like make them dinner, get them a gift, or spend the day with them, etc.) Plan a time and day to give or send this person the letter.

NOTES

Restoration

OF ALL THINGS

WEEK 7 **ON EARTH AS IT IS IN HEAVEN**

Over the past six weeks we have looked closely at the first three values of a sustainable spirituality. **Authenticity** explored how you relate to yourself in all your broken and glorious humanity as a lost and found child of God. **Intimacy** looked at how you relate to God as your loving heavenly Father. **Love** unpacked how you relate to each other as human incarnations of God's Son. Now, **Restoration** describes how you relate to the world as God's beautiful, though broken, creation needing to be renewed and managed according to God's design!

Many people grew up thinking the Bible was *a heaven and hell story.* It's all about telling you how to go to the first place and avoid the second one. Eternal life, they were told, is what happens after this life. The goal is to get "saved" and escape to heaven before God condemns the earth and sends all the wicked people in it to hell. By believing the right things about Jesus and saying the "sinner's prayer", Saint Peter will put you on God's heavenly guest list and let you through the pearly gates when you die. Then you will spend eternity singing and playing a harp while sitting on a cloud at a toga party in the sky.

This is a bit of a parody, but only slightly so. It's no wonder people have given up on Christianity with that uninspiring story that misses the point of the Bible. That distorted story trivializes this life and this world God has created, robbing us of our future hope. Thank God it's not the real story of the Bible!

The Bible is *a heaven and earth story.* It starts with God creating the heavens and the earth and declaring they are good in the beginning. It ends with heaven and earth reunited and restored. In between there is a lot of mayhem and detours, but we must not lose the plot!

Jesus declares at the end of the book, "Behold, I am making all things new." (Rev. 21:5) The New Jerusalem comes down out of heaven from God to the earth. The nations walk by its light. The rulers of the earth bring their glory into it. God is with his people with no need of a temple. The tree leaves heal the nations and the living water refreshes everything. It is as the prophets had promised, "The knowledge of God covers the earth like the waters cover the seas." (Habakkuk. 2:14, Isaiah 11:9) There is harmony again between people and animals, with humans ruling wisely as God's image bearing children. (Is. 11:6-9) This is what the world has been waiting for! (Romans. 8:18-25) It's what it is waiting for now.

But the restoration is underway! From the moment our representative ancestors went astray in the garden, God promised to destroy evil and re-establish a good human representative to rule the world. He chose one family through whom to bring that promise to fruition. Eve's descendant would be the one to crush evil and take back rightful human authority over the world. Abraham's descendant would be the one through whom all the nations of the earth would be blessed. David's descendant would sit on an eternal throne and bring justice to the whole world. Mary's son would be the one we were waiting for.

Jesus was the one referred to. He was God in the flesh. As God had humbled himself to live in a tent and a temple in the past, now he lived in one man who showed us what God is like. He went around destroying evil and all its collateral damage. He took authority over creation: stopping storms, walking on water, multiplying food, and transforming water into wine. He even defied death by raising a few people to life. These were all signs that God's Son had come to establish God's kingdom.

But Jesus said the kingdom would not come all at once or through political means. It would come subtly, gradually -- like weeds that take over a field or yeast that leavens a batch of dough. He taught his disciples to pray for God's kingdom to come and will to be done *"on earth"* as it is in heaven. The hope Jesus pointed to throughout his ministry was resurrection. God would raise the dead and restore the earth with his sons and daughters sitting on thrones to rule the place!

As the prophets said, Jesus is the king whose kingdom continues to increase forever! All other kingdoms come and go. They rise and fall. His only rises and expands until the whole creation is made new. To be Jesus' disciple is to follow him and learn to rule! We bring everything under our authority under his authority and we implement his rule in our lives as in heaven. So rather than helping us escape earth, God empowers us to join him in redeeming it!

This too is an inside-out process. As you obey his will and seek his kingdom, you can influence your family, your business and everything under your authority. Then you can influence your city, your state, your nation and your world. It always starts with the individual and moves outward. This is the mindset of hope and vision that we are describing when we talk about the restoration of all things. God is restoring all of heaven and earth starting with you!

GROUP DISCUSSION

1. What stood out to you in this reading? What did you find confusing or difficult?

2. How would you describe "the restoration of all things" in your own words?

3. What do you think the restoration of all things being an "inside-out process" means?

4. How have you seen this "inside-out process" work within people? Within communities?

5. How would you like to see the world around you restored? How would you like to partner with God in that restoration?

NOTES

WEEK 7 **DAILY DEVOTIONS**

DAY ONE
RESTORATION CLOSE TO HOME

When we think about restoration, we often jump so quickly to changing the world at large that we forget to ask how God might want to change the world close around us. There may be places that restoration can take further hold in our friendships, families, and even our own hearts.

Ask God where he wants to bring further restoration in the areas listed below. Be sure to spend a few minutes listening for his answer to each area of your life, writing down what comes to your mind and heart. Once finished, go through what you wrote down with God, asking him how his restoration might take hold in those areas. Ask him how you might partner with him in these areas of restoration.

God, where do you want to bring further restoration in my:

- **Heart**
- **Family**
- **Friendships**
- **Church**
- **Work**

NOTES

PRAYING FOR YOUR CITY

Though it may never cross your mind, praying for the city that you live in can have a huge impact for God's kingdom. A city is more than just a zip code, a collection of streets, or local laws and policies. A city is a collection of neighbors, and we know how God calls us to treat our neighbors.

Spend some time praying for the people in your local neighborhoods, schools, government, and churches. Pray that God's kingdom come and will be done in your city as it is in heaven. Ask him how you might be a part of the restoration of the place you live. Consider setting a weekly alarm on your phone reminding you to say a brief prayer for your city. Make sure that it is set for a time and day that you usually have a free moment.

_____

NOTES

NOTES

STEWARDSHIP

Stewardship is management. A steward is a house manager who manages all the finances and affairs of his or her master. Adam and Eve were given stewardship over the earth. Joseph was a steward in Potiphar's house. Jesus told stories about stewards. You are a steward of your life and everything God has entrusted to you. If you are faithful with what he has given you, he will entrust you with more. If you are a slacker, he will get someone else to do the job. (Luke 12:42-48).

Take an inventory of all God has entrusted to you. How are you managing it? How can you better leverage your time, talents and treasure to help expand God's kingdom? Are there areas where you are squandering your master's property? What would a faithful steward do if he was entrusted with your abilities, your money and your time?

NOTES

NOTES

DAY FOUR

ECOLOGY AND CREATION CARE

This restoration God is after includes the whole world. Humans were given responsibility in the garden to work it and keep it. Similarly, we are called to rule the earth and subdue it and manage it. God's restoration has always been moving forward in the direction of a city, but one that has trees and a crystal clear river and flourishing life.

How can we care for our world as stewards of creation? What is our role as Christians in caring for the earth? How can we work for better policies in our companies and our government to better care for the good world God loves?

———

NOTES

NOTES

DAY FIVE
SWEET SPOT

"We are God's workmanship, created in Christ Jesus, to do good works which God prepared in advance for us to do." (Ephesians 2:10)

How do you find that unique work God created for you to do? That thing that all your life experiences and desires have been preparing you for and pointing you to? That gift that you were created to be for the world? That way God displays his glory through you?

Your sweet spot is where what you love, what you are good at and what the world needs intersect. If you can find a way to get paid for it, you have a career. But even if you don't, you have found your calling.

Part of the unique way we each contribute to the restoration of all things is through doing meaningful work. What are you good at that you love to do? How can you use what you love and do well to meet real needs in the world? Journal on that for a while. Maybe you should ask someone else if you get stuck. Let it be an opening to find your greatest calling.

NOTES

WEEK 8 **HOME**

The Longing for Home
If you had even a marginally good childhood, "home" was imprinted on you. The longing for home is embedded somewhere deep in your spirit. In difficult times, it comes up from the depths of you like a long forgotten song lyric. No matter how content with our current life, each of us has a restlessness for a deeper home. We long for a more secure comfort and a more permanent rest.

Our True Home
Many of us have supposed that our real home is in Heaven. We are partially right. But many have made a wrong turn in thinking that our hope is to escape from this world to somewhere else. Bible verses that talk about being aliens and exiles or looking for an enduring city have led some to think that we must go somewhere else, but those same passages say that the city (the New Jerusalem) is coming here and our king is returning here! (Hebrews 13:14; 1 Peter 2:11) The Bible is about Heaven coming down to earth, rather than us going away to Heaven.

The "going somewhere else" view has been so embedded in popular culture that the true Biblical view seems strange. But once you see it, your understanding of the plot of scripture will open your eyes to hope! **God made a good world, and Jesus came to save it.** He will come back with all of Heaven (and all who have gone there ahead of us) to restore everything to its God intended glory.

The Story of Exile

The story of the Bible is built around this homeless exile. Most scholars agree that most of the Old Testament we have today was collected and compiled during the exile of the Jewish people in Babylon and addresses the question the Israelites were asking: "How did we get here and how do we get home?"

Exiled from the garden, humans end up in Babylon.

Exiled from the promised land, Israel ends up in Babylon.

Exiled from his own temple, God is killed by Babylon. (Well, technically Rome, but you get the picture!)

Home but not Home
When Jesus showed up, though some of the Jewish people had come back to the promised land and rebuilt the temple in Jerusalem, many people sensed God's glory had never returned to fill the temple. It seemed God was missing and the Romans were ruling. Though technically home, Israelites were still in occupied territory. The exile continued.

But God had promised to return to his people. In Jesus he did. He personally fulfilled his promise about a descendent of Eve (Genesis 3), and from Abraham (Genesis 15). God is faithful even when we are not. He makes his home WITH his people and IN those who trust in him. We are the new temple. He has made his home with us. And while the presence of his Spirit in us is just a deposit on our future inheritance, it is a great start!

"Now we are a kingdom of priests and a holy nation, a people belonging to God." (1 Peter 2:9). Now we get to represent God to the people around us by loving and blessing them in the name of Jesus. And we get to represent those people to God by praying for them and interceding for them. We are the connection between heaven and earth. We are the true temple of God. We are his home and he is ours. We live in him and he lives in us. This is where "on earth as in heaven" begins.

But it must continue outward from us. The restoration of all things is underway, but it will not be complete until every knee bows and tongue confesses Jesus as Lord. We each have a part to play in God's restoration project within our spheres of influence. Restoration is happening and restoration is coming. Heaven is invading earth in us and through us. That's why we pray together with our brothers and sisters all over the world:

'Our Father in heaven, hallowed be your name, your kingdom come, your will be done, on earth as it is in heaven. Give us today our daily bread. And forgive us our debts, as we also have forgiven our debtors. And lead us not into temptation, but deliver us from evil. For yours is the kingdom and the power and the glory forever. Amen.'

Briefly discuss the above reading and what stands out to you? Be sure to leave enough time for the Group Experience below.

GROUP EXPERIENCE:

Supplies:
- One index card per person
- Pens
- Phone timer

The Goal:

The goal of this activity is to get you thinking and praying about how you have been impacted by God during this eight week experience AND how you and your group can join in God's restorative work as you move into the future.

Instructions:
Pass out an index card to each person. On one side of your card write the words **"God, you have shown me..."** at the top. On the other side write **"God, you are calling me..."** at the top. Then spend five minutes individually praying, asking God to help you answer the following two questions:

"God, what have you shown me in this eight week experience that you want me to hold on to?"

"God, how are you calling me to join you in your restorative work in the world around me?"

Then take turns having each person share what they heard and wrote down on both sides of their card and why. After each person has shared, give an opportunity for others to encourage and affirm the person who shared.

Finally, pray for that member of the group committing them to the restorative work to which God is calling them. When you have finished with every member pray a prayer for your group as you finish your experience.

THINGS TO REMEMBER:

- Remember this is just a conversation with God. There is no need to put a lot of pressure on yourself to find the "right" answer.

- This is an activity that you and God can do together. As you are praying, pay attention to what he might bring to your mind and impress on your heart.

- If you are unsure of what God is saying, what do you think God might say?

- Don't feel pressured to write down fully-formed thoughts. God can sometimes speak to us in words, phrases, or pictures that are not fully fleshed out in the moment. And that's okay!

- Prayers for others do not have to be long to be powerful. Make sure you leave enough time for every member of the group to share and be prayed for.

BEFORE FINISHING YOUR TIME TOGETHER BE SURE TO READ THE SO WHAT'S NEXT? SECTION ON THE NEXT PAGE.

SO WHAT'S NEXT?

BEYOND WEEK 8 **WAYS TO KEEP SUSTAINING**

When a tree is young it is sometimes accompanied by a narrow wooden stake, anchored in the ground near its roots and strapped to its trunk. This stake is there to help the young tree grow straight and upright which it would not have the strength to do on its own. We hope that this eight-week experience has functioned in much the same way, providing structure, guidance, and strength to support you on a journey of sustainable spirituality.

We also recognize that, like the tree, relying on this structure too long can have negative consequences. A tree that relies on the stake too long can become weak and dependent. To have a sustainable spirituality, there comes a time to pull the stake and allow God to bring about new ways to grow you in faith, hope and love.

This does not mean that you are then on your own, relying on your own fortitude. God desires that we all learn to walk side by side with him and trust in his strength more and more. Further, the relationships you have made in the last eight weeks are there to support, encourage, and care for you. You can also find further guidance, care, training, and resources at your local church to help enhance your continued experience in community and as an individual. To "pull the stake" simply means that it is time for your relationship with God and others to grow deeper and richer than what you have experienced over the past eight weeks. Like a thriving tree doing what it was designed to do: Grow!

Check out these helpful tips to continue sustaining what God has planted:

SUSTAIN IN COMMUNITY

At your last meeting take some time to discuss what the future of your group looks like. Here are some tips that might help:

- **Be friends:** Don't let your group become just another church program. Programs rarely last. Friendships often do. Hang together, eat together, have fun together, and live normal life in relationship outside of your weekly meeting time. Don't wait for someone else to reach out. If you all initiate your chances of lasting friendship will increase substantially.

- **Be intentional:** Continue the intentionality that you have been practicing the last eight weeks. Pray for each other's needs. Encourage one another regularly. Have honest conversations about what's really going on. Keep talking about God, his word, and how that impacts your lives. A little intentionality can immensely boost the value of your relationships.

- **Be realistic:** The best plan is the one you will actually follow through with. If meeting once a week is too much for you to handle, try once or twice a month. The important thing is that you continue meeting regularly. Find what works best for your group.

- **Be Organized:** Plan out your schedules carefully so

that busyness does not get in the way of great community. Organize plans for your next meeting in person while you are all still together. It is much harder to organize at a later time through email, text, or social media. Organization is not the goal. It is simply a helpful tool.

- **Be restorers:** As a group, join in God's restoration of the world around you. Keep praying about and dreaming of what God is calling you to as a group. Find ways to serve together. Put together a party and invite your neighbors. Find a ministry or cause to support as a group. Help God's kingdom come in your neighborhood as it is in heaven.

SUSTAIN PERSONALLY

Beyond your group, we hope that you will continue to develop a sustainable and continually growing spirituality on a personal level. Remember the things that you do to nurture your relationship with Jesus are about living out the full life he offers you, not about dutifully trying to please. Here are some ways to open up to him and the life he offers:

- **Find prayer that sustains you:** Prayer simply describes our interaction and communication with God. Some people approach prayer with shame, insecurity, or duty because of many misconceptions. If we can put those falsities aside, however, we will see how God simply desires to connect with us, care for our needs, and have us enjoy his transformative presence. Our journey then becomes one of learning how you and God best communicate with each other. Trying lots of different methods of prayer can help you hone in on what a healthy prayer life is for you. Check out our **Thoughts on Prayer** section on page 141.

- **Read the Bible as food for your soul:** God has given us an incredible life - giving resource that is his written word, the Bible. Spending time reading it will help nourish your life. Whether you are a seasoned scholar of the scripture or new to this whole Bible-thing, the Holy Spirit can speak to you powerfully through the Bible. Learn to look to it as a blessing to your soul. Unsure where to start or just looking to beef up your Bible knowledge? Try reading through a book at a time using the helpful resources at www.thebibleproject.com to guide you.

- **Spiritual direction and mentorship:** Spiritual directors have been used by believers for centuries as a means of guidance, wisdom, and soul care. A director is a trained spiritual companion who walks alongside you as you seek to walk with God. He or she meets regularly with you to listen to God alongside you concerning your spiritual journey. A typical direction session lasts an hour and involves sharing, listening, and praying. An untrained spiritual mentor can also be a great blessing to you. Just ask the identified person if he or she would like to mentor you and then set up a time to meet regularly. Gleaning the wisdom and guidance of someone who is a few (or maybe many) steps ahead of you can make a huge difference in your spiritual journey. Looking for a spiritual director near you? Check out these websites: www.soulshepherding.org | www.be.org

- **Spiritual practices that open your heart:** There are many incredible practices (both new and old) that can be used as tools to open your heart to God. It is important to note that these practices, often referred to as spiritual disciplines, are not powerful in and of themselves, but can be helpful in opening our hearts to God's power. Want to learn more about spiritual disciplines? Check out the **List of Spiritual Disciplines** on page 143.

- **Have a STAKE in your church:** You are not just an attender of your church, you are a part of it. The church is not a time, organization, or place. It is a community of people. Have a S.T.A.K.E in that community. (i.e., serve according to your gifts, tithe according to your means, attend and engage regularly, keep the unity of the church a priority, and embody the values of your church in your neighborhood.

There are more resources to refer to in the back of this Guidebook. Check them out now and come back to them as much as you need.

EXTRAS

THOUGHTS ON PRAYER

THE HEART OF PRAYER
LEARNING FROM JESUS

Many of us approach prayer with fear of inadequacy or looking foolish. It is common to think "I don't know how to pray," or "I am not good at praying." But when we take a few moments to understand the gift of prayer and what it is meant for, this intimidation factor can fade and give way to a life-changing and fruitful connection.

Jesus actually addresses many misconceptions about prayer that still exist today. (Matthew 6:5-13) He points out that prayer shouldn't be about impressing others, saying the right thing, or using the most words. Though it is appropriate at times to have extended, eloquent, or even public prayers, many who were practicing these forms of prayer in Jesus' day had forgotten or ignored why the gift of prayer exists in the first place. They made it about a show or saying the magic words, but Jesus wanted his disciples to understand what prayer was really about.

He points out that "your Father knows what you need before you ask him." (Matthew 6:8) So why do we pray at all? Why doesn't God just anticipate our needs and provide for us accordingly? That's because prayer first and foremost is about fostering our relationship with God. He wants a connection with us, both because he loves us and knows how good it is for us to spend time with him. And this takes the pressure off of prayer, leaving us to just be ourselves with God.

AUTHENTICITY IN PRAYER

Though it sounds simple enough, we can still run into roadblocks when it comes to our prayer lives. We can have times where we feel lost, confused, or even alone in our prayers. Other times we feel too ashamed to speak to God and feel as though we need to somehow clean ourselves up beforehand. In these seasons it is all the more important for us to lean into authenticity with ourselves and God. If we want a helpful model for authentic prayer we need look no further than the Psalms.

The Psalms are filled with beautiful and uplifting prayers that we love to quote and hang on our walls. However, they are also filled with the dark depths of human emotion. Sometimes in that same psalm you will find beautiful declarations of faith and the beauty of God's love, side-by-side with the Psalmist's declaration of hate for his enemies and his desire that God would slay them all. The contrast is almost comical at times.

That is because authenticity (as covered in weeks 1 and 2) is both about the truth of who you are *and* where you are at. God wants to hear all of what you are feeling and experiencing, while at the same time wanting you to remember the truth of who he is and who you are in his eyes. It can be easy to embrace one without the other. We can declare all the truths of who we are and how we love God, but if we are never real with him about where we are, we miss an important aspect of connecting with God. In the same way, if in prayer we only focus on where we are at in the moment, we can become convinced that where we are is who we are. We must balance both in our prayer life if we are to work toward true authentic relationship.

LIST OF SPIRITUAL DISCIPLINES

SOME THINGS TO TRY
A NONCOMPREHENSIVE LIST

Check out this list of spiritual disciplines on the next page. Keep in mind that there is no comprehensive list. A discipline[1] is simply any practice that helps to open your heart to God. You probably already engage in many without even realizing it (such as worshiping through music, spending time in Christ-centered community, serving others in tangible ways, or going away on a church retreat every year).

The list below can be your starting place to incorporate some new and helpful disciplines into your life, but don't be afraid to try more unconventional disciplines too (or even create your own). There are some who pray on their commute to work rather than listen to radio, use speed bumps as a reminder to slow down and be with God, and even pray for friends as they pop up on their social media feed. Balance both pushing yourself and finding what works for you.

---

1. *Don't let the word "discipline" throw you off. It has nothing to do with punishment. A discipline is simply a practice to which you commit. Think of it as a spiritual practice you are committing yourself to try.*

DISCIPLINES OF ENGAGEMENT[2]

These are ways of connecting with God and other people, conversing honestly with them in order to love and be loved.

- **Bible Reading:** Trusting the Holy Spirit-inspired words of Scripture as our guide, wisdom, and strength for life. (Related disciplines include Bible study, Scripture meditation, and praying God's Word.)

- **Worship:** Praising God's greatness, goodness, and beauty in words, music, ritual, or silence. (We can worship God privately or in community.)

- **Prayer:** Conversing with God about what we're experiencing and doing together. (As we see in the Lord's Prayer the main thing we do in prayer is to make requests or intercessions to our Father for one another.)

- **Soul Friendship:** Engaging fellow disciples of Jesus in prayerful conversation or other spiritual practices. (Related spiritual disciplines or practices include small groups, spiritual direction, and mentoring relationships.)

- **Personal Reflection:** Paying attention to our inner self in order to grow in love for God, others, and self. (The Psalms in the Bible model this.)

- **Service:** Humbly serving God by overflowing with his love and compassion to others, especially those in need. (Also tithing and giving.)

---

2. *This list in its entirerty is courtesy of SOULSHEPHERDING.COM http://www.soulshepherding.org/2012/07/spiritual-disciplines-list/*

DISCIPLINES OF ABSTINENCE

These are ways of denying ourselves something we want or need in order to make space to focus on and connect with God.

- **Solitude:** Finding a quiet place and refraining from interacting with other people in order to be alone with God and be found by him. (Solitude is completed by silence.)

- **Silence:** Not speaking in a place of solitude in order to quiet our minds and whole self, attend to God's presence, and listen to others in order to bless them.

- **Fasting:** Going without food (or something else like TV or other media) for a period of intensive prayer — the fast may be complete or partial.

- **Sabbath:** Doing no work to rest in God's person and provision; praying and playing with God and others. (God designed this for one day a week. We can practice it for shorter periods too.)

- **Secrecy:** Not making our good deeds or qualities known in order to let God or others receive attention and to find our sufficiency in God alone (e.g., see Matthew 6).

- **Submission:** Not asserting ourselves in order to come under the authority, wisdom, and power of Jesus Christ as our Lord, King, and Master. (If you think of this as submitting to another person as unto Christ then it's a discipline of engagement.)

A FEW MORE THINGS
TO KEEP IN MIND

As you dive into the practice of spiritual disciplines there are a couple things to keep in mind.

- **Spiritual Disciplines Are Not Law:** There is no biblical mandate that we practice spiritual disciplines. Rather they are a tool that we can choose to use as a way of greater openness and connection with God. They are made to serve us, we are not made to serve them. This frees us up to not worry when we fail or struggle with a discipline. In fact, the more you struggle with a discipline, the more helpful it will likely be to you.

- **Spiritual Disciplines Are Not Formulaic:** Like so many other things in life spiritual disciplines do not guarantee success in every spiritual venture. You cannot check them off like a list of "to-do's" and expect transformation. Like all forms of training, they are helpful in putting you in the best position to grow in relationship with God. Think of it as tending to the soil of your own heart so that it is more ready to receive what God has to offer.

- **Spiritual Disciplines Are Not Transformative:** This bears repeating. If you trust in spiritual disciplines to transform you, you will be vastly disappointed. Spiritual disciplines are helpful tools in opening our heart to the only one who can transform us, Jesus. Remember that our goal in spiritual disciplines is a greater connection with him!

NOTES

NOTES

NOTES

NOTES